"WHEN I OPENED MY MOUTH TO SING, IT WAS THERE, A FEELING AND A SPIRIT THAT WOULD COME THROUGH ME AND OUT OF MY MOUTH. IT WASN'T ANYTHING I COULD CONTROL. I DIDN'T FIGHT IT. IT WAS JUST THERE."

WHITNEY HOUSTON

1963–2012

WHITNEY HOUSTON

RECORDING ARTIST & ACTRESS

BY CHRISTINE HEPPERMANN

CREDITS

Published by ABDO Publishing Company, PO Box 398166, Minneapolis, MN 55439. Copyright © 2013 by Abdo Consulting Group, Inc. International copyrights reserved in all countries. No part of this book may be reproduced in any form without written permission from the publisher. The Essential Library™ is a trademark and logo of ABDO Publishing Company.

Printed in the United States of America, North Mankato, Minnesota
062012
022013

Editor: Melissa York
Series Designer: Becky Daum

Library of Congress Cataloging-in-Publication Data
Heppermann, Christine.
  Whitney Houston : recording artist & actress / Christine Heppermann.
      p. cm. -- (Lives cut short)
  Includes bibliographical references.
  ISBN 978-1-61783-544-5
  1. Houston, Whitney--Juvenile literature. 2. Singers--United States--Biography--Juvenile literature. 3. Motion picture actors and actresses--United States--Biography--Juvenile literature. I. Title.
  ML3930.H7H46 2013
  782.42164'092--dc23
  [B]
                                        2012018442

TABLE OF CONTENTS

1

AMERICA'S
SWEETHEART

umping one fist into the air and then the other, Whitney Houston held the last note of the "Star-Spangled Banner." Her voice soared above the cheers of the crowd into the hazy Florida sky, where a formation of F-16 jets streaked over Tampa Stadium for a dramatic grand finale.

"It was the most electric moment that I have ever seen in sports," recalled sportscaster Frank Gifford, and many people agree with him.[1] Of all the things Americans may have forgotten about

▸ WHITNEY HOUSTON'S PERFORMANCE AT THE 1991 SUPER BOWL IS CONSIDERED ONE OF THE BEST EVER.

the Super Bowl XXV matchup between the New York Giants and the Buffalo Bills on January 27, 1991—which team won (the Giants), or which band performed in the halftime show (New Kids on the Block)—most have not forgotten Houston's stirring gospel-and-jazz-influenced rendition of the national anthem.

Though Houston was a pop music superstar, she was not dressed like one that day. She wore a modest white nylon tracksuit with a white band holding back her hair. Accompanied by the Florida Orchestra, she got up to the microphone before the game and gave it her all. *Los Angeles Times* sports columnist J. A. Adande listed her "Star-Spangled Banner" as one of his all-time favorite performances of the song. As he explained, "It dripped red, white, and blue."[2]

Lip-Synching Controversy

The Super Bowl audience heard Houston's voice, but she was not singing live. Instead, she was lip-synching to the "protection copy," a version of the song the National Football League (NFL) required her to pre-record in a studio in case she became sick with laryngitis or had other voice troubles on game day. Although Houston received some criticism after news of her lip-synching spread through the media, it is fairly common for singers to prerecord their performances of the national anthem because many things can go wrong. For example, in 2011, singer Christina Aguilera forgot some of the song's lyrics when she risked a live performance at Super Bowl XLV. The next day, she issued a formal apology, saying, "I only hope that everyone could feel my love for this country."[3]

WARTIME PERFORMANCE

Only ten days earlier, on January 17, the United States had entered the Persian Gulf War in reaction to Iraq's invasion of Kuwait. Thus, the words of the national anthem held extra significance for the 73,813 fans in the stadium—many waving tiny US flags—and the millions more watching on television. Lined up across the football field stood men and women from the different branches of the US military, each holding a flag from one of the 50 states. In an atmosphere so charged with patriotism, Houston knew she needed to deliver something extra special. She later told a reporter from *People* magazine, "I remember standing there and looking at all those people, and it was like I could see in their faces the hopes and prayers and fears of the entire country."[4]

Certainly by this stage of her career, Houston was well accustomed to dazzling audiences with her powerful mezzo-soprano voice. At 27, she had three hugely successful studio albums and

Encore

Houston sang at the Super Bowl to honor the troops overseas, and she sang for them when they came home. On March 31, 1991, Houston performed a live televised concert, *Welcome Home Heroes with Whitney Houston*, in an airplane hangar at Virginia's Norfolk Naval Air Station before a crowd of Gulf War veterans and their families. Fans loved her rendition of the "Star-Spangled Banner," as well as performances of her other hit love songs.

a record-holding seven consecutive Number 1 hit singles, besting the old record of six shared by British pop group the Beatles and Australian group the Bee Gees. Yet on Super Bowl Sunday, when she finished the song and went up to a skybox to watch the game, she did not immediately realize how big an impression her performance had made.

The next day, Houston's recording label, Arista Records, received a flood of requests from callers desperate to buy a copy of the song. And the requests did not slow. Apparently, for legions of

What Is a Recording Label?

A recording label, or record label, pays to have an artist's music produced, distributed to radio stations and retailers, and marketed to the public. The label then earns money by taking a share of the artist's profits. Within a major record label such as Arista (which today is part of a larger corporation, BMG, that owns multiple labels), there are different departments. Employees in the A and R (artists and repertory) department scout for new talent and guide artists through the recording process. The art department designs album covers and promotional materials. The marketing department coordinates advertising campaigns and works with the publicity, promotion, and sales departments to make sure an artist's music is being played on the radio, talked about in the media, and sold in stores. Other record label departments include legal, business, and, more recently, new media, which is in charge of maintaining an artist's presence on the Internet. A company president oversees the whole process, making sure all departments do their best to help artists—and thus the label—achieve success.

listeners, once was not enough. They wanted to hear Houston sing the "Star-Spangled Banner" over and over again.

A few weeks later, Arista released the song on video and as a single, and it became the company's fastest-selling single ever. In a matter of weeks, sales added up to more than $500,000. At Houston's request, all proceeds from the single went to an American Red Cross fund to aid Gulf War soldiers and their families.

RERELEASE

Ten years later, Arista rereleased the single after the September 11, 2001, terrorist attacks on New York City and Washington DC, and it climbed to Number 6 on the *Billboard* pop chart. Again, all profits were donated to charity, but this time the money went to relief funds for New York City firefighters and police officers. There was talk about how wonderful it would be if Houston could once again comfort the nation in a time of crisis by singing the national anthem at the first Super Bowl following the attacks, Super Bowl XXXVI.

But that honor ultimately went to another singer, Mariah Carey, because Houston's reputation had changed since 1991. Her image as the perfect all-American girl had become

▲ HOUSTON RECEIVED A LIFETIME ACHIEVEMENT AWARD
FROM TELEVISION NETWORK BET IN 2001.

tarnished by erratic behavior. She canceled
concerts at the last minute. She arrived hours late
for interviews and other scheduled appearances
and then often acted bizarrely when she finally
did show up. Rumors circulated that she and
her husband, R&B singer Bobby Brown, were

using drugs. In January 2000, security personnel stopped the couple at a Hawaii airport. The officers reportedly found marijuana in Houston's carry-on bag, but she and Brown boarded their plane to San Francisco, California, before the police arrived. Charges were subsequently dropped.

However, it appeared as if Houston's career was as healthy as ever. Her *Whitney: The Greatest Hits* album, which included the "Star-Spangled Banner," had been released in May 2000, reaching Number 1 on the pop charts and going on to sell more than 10 million copies worldwide. She renewed her recording contract with Arista for $100 million in August 2001. It was the biggest record deal in music history to that date.

Still, Houston was more than just a music industry powerhouse. She was more than her golden voice and more than America's sweetheart. She was a real person, a girl from New Jersey who had weaknesses as well as strengths, just like anybody else.

———•◆•———

2

NIPPY

Whitney Houston was born into a musical family. Her mother, Cissy Houston (born Emily Drinkard), had a busy career as a backup singer. During the summer of 1963, while pregnant with her third child, Cissy spent long hours at the Atlantic Records studio in New York City. There, she recorded vocal tracks for albums by Aretha Franklin, Wilson Pickett, and other popular singers of the day. She worked right past her baby's due date, making her boss Tom

Dowd, Atlantic Records' chief engineer, extremely nervous. As Cissy recalled,

> *The baby was overdue, I was huge and I'd get these false labor pains. Tom would stop the session, petrified I was going to have the baby right in the studio.* [1]

On August 9, 1963, at a hospital in Newark, New Jersey, Cissy gave birth to a daughter and named her Whitney Elizabeth—"Whitney" after a character on one of her favorite television shows and "Elizabeth" after her husband John Houston's mother. Baby Whitney soon acquired a nickname too. Her father, noting the stubborn way she kicked off her blankets the moment after he tucked her in, decided she reminded him of

Aretha Franklin

Born in 1942, Aretha Louise Franklin grew up singing and playing piano in Detroit's New Bethel Baptist Church, where her father, Reverend C. L. Franklin, was the minister. Reverend Franklin also traveled the country preaching, and the teenage Aretha went with him to sing gospel during his services. Having made her first gospel recording at age 14, she later branched into R&B in 1960, signing with Columbia Records. But she never abandoned her gospel roots. Well known for her rousing gospel-influenced hit song "Respect," Franklin had won 18 Grammy Awards as of 2012 and was the first female artist to be inducted into the Rock and Roll Hall of Fame. Cissy Houston's backup group, the Sweet Inspirations, often accompanied Franklin in concert and on her albums.

the comic strip character Nippy, who always got into trouble.

Baby Nippy joined two older siblings, half-brother Gary and brother Michael, at the family's third-floor apartment in Newark. She quickly became a daddy's girl. Because Cissy earned good money as a backup singer, the couple decided that John, who worked on and off as a truck driver, would stay home to take care of the children. It was John who brushed Whitney's hair, helped her dress for school, cooked family dinners, and, by his own admission, spoiled his precious only daughter. As he recalled,

> *Nippy was so bad . . . Nippy was terrible! And I loved her to death. I had waited all my life for a girl child and when I got her . . . she was something, boy, she was something else.*[2]

Cissy sometimes brought her daughter along with her to the studio to watch recording sessions. Years later, Whitney said that, thanks to her mother's career, she grew up in "an atmosphere of total creativity."[3]

A MUSICAL CHILDHOOD
Musical talent certainly ran in Cissy's side of the family. Since childhood, Cissy had sung with her brothers and sisters in a respected gospel

group, the Drinkard Singers. Cissy also sang with Whitney's first cousin Dionne Warwick and Dionne's sister Dee Dee in a different gospel group, the Gospelaires. Then, in the 1960s, Warwick transitioned into pop and contemporary music, becoming a successful solo artist. Additionally, though not related by blood, Franklin, who is often called the "Queen of Soul," was an influential presence in young Whitney's life. Whitney called her "Auntie Ree."

Given her background, it was inevitable Whitney would sing in church, especially since Cissy directed the choirs at Newark's New Hope Baptist Church, the Houston family's place of worship. New Hope became a haven for Nippy when she had trouble at school. The Houstons had moved to East Orange, a suburb of Newark, in 1967, and Whitney had a hard time making friends. For one thing, she dressed differently than most of the kids in her class. Cissy wanted her daughter to look nice, so she bought her beautiful outfits that stood out against

Dionne Warwick

Dionne Warwick is the daughter of Cissy's oldest sister Lee. Her last name was actually Warrick. Supposedly, the record company misprinted it as Warwick on her first single in 1962, "Don't Make Me Over," and she has kept it that way ever since. Since the 1960s, 56 of her singles have made the *Billboard Hot 100* chart, which is more than any other female vocalist except Aretha Franklin.

the casual fashions of her peers. Whitney remembered,

> *The other girls were dressing down with their jeans and stuff, and there I was with my plaid skirt, bucks, and pigtails. . . . At the age of ten, I was already a marked woman.*[4]

Girls chased her and called her names, so her mother gave her this advice: "Whitney, sometimes you just have to be your own best friend. Sometimes you're better off just being by yourself."[5] Still, Cissy did not want her daughter sitting around the house alone, moping. So she brought her to choir practice.

Whitney had different ideas about what she wanted to be when she grew up. She wanted to be a teacher or a veterinarian. Then, when she was 11, she performed her first solo, the gospel hymn "Guide Me, O Thou Great Jehovah," at a Sunday service. Her voice brought the congregation to tears. From that day forward, she knew what she wanted to be: a singer.

The Drinkard Singers

Cissy and her brothers Nicky and Larry and sisters Lee, Marie, Anne, and Judy first started singing for fun at home. Their father started them rehearsing seriously in 1938, when Cissy was five years old, and they went from clowning around in the living room to singing in church to performing with legendary gospel singer Mahalia Jackson at Carnegie Hall in 1951. The Drinkard Singers recorded three albums, starting with *A Joyful Noise* in 1958.

▲ WHITNEY LEARNED TO SING IN THE NEW HOPE BAPTIST CHURCH GOSPEL CHOIR.

Remembering all her years singing in choir, Whitney said,

> *While serving my apprenticeship in that choir, I learned everything I needed to know about singing: how to sing when the tempo changes in the middle of a song, how to sing four-part harmony without even thinking about it twice and how to sing a cappella, which is the greatest school of all—your voice is the instrument, your feet are the drum and your hands are the tambourine.[6]*

A START IN MODELING

By the late 1970s, Nippy
was tagging along with
Cissy to cabarets and clubs
in New York City, and the
two sometimes sang duets
together. During one such
mother-daughter performance
at Carnegie Hall in 1978,
a photographer from *Vogue*
magazine was in the audience.
After the show, he approached
15-year-old Whitney to ask if she had ever
considered modeling. She soon signed with a
modeling agency and began traveling regularly to
New York City to do photo shoots for magazines
such as *Vogue*, *Cosmopolitan*, *Glamour*, and
Seventeen. In November 1981, she became the
second African-American model ever to appear
on *Seventeen*'s cover. The cover photo shows her
in a white sweaterdress and matching tights,
eating a triple-decker ice cream cone and giggling
with the model seated next to her. She is the ideal
picture of a happy, carefree, all-American girl.

Her parents wanted to make sure she stayed
a happy, normal teenager for as long as possible.
They wanted her to finish high school at Mount

Secret Code

Gospel music has roots in
African-American spirituals,
which are religious hymns
slaves sang to lift their spir-
its and help them face their
difficult lives. Often these
spirituals included secret
antislavery messages. For
instance, "Moses" was code
for Harriet Tubman, founder
of the Underground Rail-
road that guided slaves to
freedom in the North.

▲ WHITNEY'S SENIOR YEARBOOK PHOTO

Saint Dominic's Academy, an all-girl Catholic school, before signing with a record company. Whitney brought her homework with her when she went on photo shoots or singing gigs. Cissy knew from personal experience how tough the music industry could be, and she wanted her daughter to hold on to her childhood for as long as possible.

RECORDING CONTRACT

Houston's entry into show business followed a similar pattern to her mother's. She started off singing backup vocals for pop and R&B acts such as Chaka Khan, Jermaine Jackson, Lou Rawls, and the Neville Brothers. But, with her undeniable talent, she would not stay in the background for long.

One of the industry talent scouts who first noticed Houston was Gerry Griffith from Arista Records. In 1980, he and a colleague went to a New York nightclub, the Bottom Line, to meet with a musician. While there, they caught the evening's opening act: Cissy Houston. Cissy brought her 17-year-old daughter up on stage to sing with her for one number. Whitney's voice captivated Griffith. His friend urged him to offer her a recording contract with Arista right then and there, but Griffith decided to wait. He told his friend, "As good as she is, there's still something lacking. She isn't quite ripe yet."[7]

Two years later, though, when Griffith found out that other record companies were eager to sign Houston, he went to hear her sing again at another club. She sang "Tomorrow" from the musical *Annie*, and this time her performance stunned him. As he recalled,

> *I couldn't believe she had grown so much in that two-year period. She went from a teenager to a woman . . . she had obvious star quality.*

It took no genius to see it—all you had to do was just see her and you knew.[8]

Griffith arranged an audition for Houston with his boss, Clive Davis. Houston would sing a mix of classic songs and end with "Tomorrow" as her grand finale.

Davis was the founder and president of Arista Records. He knew how to recognize talent and turn promising singers and musicians into stars. Cissy was already familiar with Davis's reputation. She trusted him from his work producing albums for Warwick and Franklin. Would he see star quality in her daughter, she wondered?

Cissy should not have worried. Thanks to Whitney's amazing ability to perform under pressure, she showed no sign of nervousness, even with the powerful Davis watching her. Plus, she impressed Griffith even further. He said,

I mean, I knew she was good, but she just put on a magnificent performance at the [audition]. Aside from the natural talent and the great looks, the lady has got guts.[9]

Whitney and her parents considered offers from several different record companies, but, in 1983, they decided to go with Arista. Davis felt confident that adding this fresh-faced 19-year-old singer to Arista's stable of artists was a smart

▲ WHITNEY AND CLIVE DAVIS WOULD FORM A LONG AND
BENEFICIAL PARTNERSHIP AND FRIENDSHIP.

decision. And taking a chance on Whitney would
turn out to be one of the smartest career moves
Davis ever made.

3

A SUPERSTAR DEBUTS

n April 29, 1983, Davis sat and chatted comfortably with talk show host Merv Griffin. As a guest on that day's episode of *The Merv Griffin Show*, Davis had brought one of Arista's newest recording artists, Houston, along with him, and he could hardly wait to introduce her to Griffin's audience. This would be Houston's first-ever televised performance. Before she came on stage, Davis described to the host what set this young lady apart from other vocalists: "It's her natural charm. You've either got it or you

▸ HOUSTON WITH HER SELF-TITLED DEBUT ALBUM IN 1984, SHORTLY BEFORE ITS RELEASE

Record Producers

A record producer is like a movie director in that he or she is responsible for the overall process of creating an album. Often, multiple producers work together on one record. For example, Davis was the executive, or main, producer on *Whitney Houston*, but he hired others to oversee the arranging and recording of individual songs. Producers can mold and shape an album to the point that the music reflects their creative vision just as much—or more—than that of the recording artist.

don't have it. She's got it."[1] Then Houston walked from the wings, dressed in a long black skirt and a shiny blue blouse with puffy sleeves, and showed everyone what Davis meant. Singing "Home" from the Wizard of Oz–inspired musical *The Wiz*, her voice started at almost a whisper and steadily gained power. When she finished, the television studio erupted in applause. Griffin walked over to greet her and announced to viewers, "You won't forget that name—Whitney Houston!"[2]

Yet Davis knew from his many years in the music business that raw talent and charisma were not enough to transform a singer into a star. That is why he and his colleagues at Arista spent more than two years putting together Whitney's first album. They flew her back and forth between New York City and Los Angeles, California, showcasing her for songwriters and producers in a hunt for material she could record. Davis wanted to find the perfect combination of songs.

He believed Houston had a real opportunity to become a crossover artist, meaning she would appeal to a wide range of listeners, white and African American, with a variety of musical tastes—pop, R&B, soul, and adult contemporary. When anyone approached Davis with a potential song for Houston to record, he had one main rule for judging it: will it be a hit?

In the end, six of the ten tracks on the self-titled album *Whitney Houston*, released in February 1985, were ballads—romantic, slow-tempo songs intended to highlight Houston's vocal range. How would these dreamy melodies compete on the radio with high-energy rock-and-roll numbers? As journalist Richard Corliss wrote in *Time*, there was no guarantee radio stations would embrace Houston's music and play it regularly: "The chanteuse [female singer] had to fight for air play with hard rockers. . . . The soul strutter had to seduce a music audience that anointed few black artists with superstardom."[3]

And seduce them she did. As of 2012, *Whitney Houston* stood as the best-selling debut album by any female recording artist in history. It sold tens of millions of copies worldwide and gave Houston a chain of hit singles, including "You Give Good Love," "Saving All My Love for

You," "How Will I Know," and "The Greatest Love of All." At the Twenty-Eighth Grammy Awards, which took place on February 25, 1986, she received a nomination for Album of the Year and took home the award for Best Pop Vocal Performance, Female for "Saving All My Love for You."

CRITICS RESPOND

Music critics praised Houston's voice, but some felt Davis played it too safe with his song selections. A reviewer for *Rolling Stone* called *Whitney Houston* a mix of "pleasant but

---

Awards

Houston received many awards and nominations for her debut album and its singles, including:

- Thirteen American Music Award nominations—still a record number for an individual album in 2012—and seven wins in categories such as Favorite Soul/R&B Single for "You Give Good Love" (1986), Favorite Pop/Rock Album (1987), and Favorite Pop/Rock Artist (1987).
- Three Grammy Award nominations and one win for Best Pop Vocal Performance, Female on "Saving All My Love for You" (1986).
- MTV Music Award for Best Female Video for "How Will I Know" (1986).
- Billboard Music Awards for New Pop Artist and New Black Artist (1985).
- Emmy Award for Outstanding Individual Performance in a Variety or Musical Program for her performance at the 28th Annual Grammy Awards (1986).
- National Association for the Advancement of Colored People (NAACP) Image Award for Outstanding New Artist (1985).

▲ HOUSTON WON HER FIRST GRAMMY AWARD IN 1986.

undistinguished pop-soul tunes."[4] Nevertheless, the review ended with this prediction: "With her sleek beauty and her great voice, Whitney Houston is obviously headed for stardom, and if nothing else, her album is an exciting preview of coming attractions."[5]

Cissy was frustrated by the response of some African-American listeners. Cissy said,

> *I found it annoying that Whitney was criticized by black critics who said her music wasn't black enough. They completely missed the point. The triumph of a Whitney Houston is that as a black performer she was allowed to record a great variety of material—not just R&B.*[6]

In addition, Houston's success opened doors for other African-American female pop singers. Music critic Dennis Hunt, writing in the *Los Angeles Times*, noted, "With one multimillion-selling album, her first—*Whitney Houston*—she made black women singers fashionable again."[7] Houston described her musical philosophy in simple terms: "I don't sing music thinking this is black or this is white. . . . I sing songs that everybody's going to like."[8]

All in the Family

As Houston's fame grew, she kept her family close. Her half brother Gary and her cousin Felicia Moss sang backup at her concerts, and Cissy often joined her daughter on stage for duets. Houston's other brother Michael acted as her road manager and traveled with her regularly, as did her best friend Robyn Crawford, whom Houston considered to be the sister she never had. Her dad John eventually took over as head of her management company, Nippy Inc., in 1989.

GROWING VISIBILITY

Not only did audiences like listening to her, they liked watching her sing and dance too. Music Television (MTV), the television network originally designed as a kind of visual radio station, increased Houston's exposure by airing her music videos frequently. Whether bopping through a colorful fun-house maze surrounded by other dancers in the video for "How Will I Know?" or crooning for the delighted kitchen staff in a closed restaurant in the video for "You Give Good Love," Houston's fresh-faced beauty and energy were mesmerizing. She did not need revealing clothes to seduce an audience, and Cissy insisted her daughter's wardrobe not be overly sexy. When managers tried to dress Houston in outfits Cissy described as "cut way up to here and way down to there," Cissy put her foot down. "From then on," Houston said, "my mother took care of my clothes."[9]

Television Roles

Though she would not appear in films until the 1990s, Houston showed up on the small screen in the 1980s with guest roles on television shows. She appeared on an episode of the situation comedy *Gimme a Break!* in 1984, and later that year, playing herself, she sang on an episode of the soap opera *As the World Turns*. In 1985, she again played herself on the situation comedy *Silver Spoons*, performing "Saving All My Love for You." Coca-Cola used her in a 1986 ad campaign for Diet Coke. She sang the "Just for the Taste of It" Diet Coke theme song in a string of popular commercials.

▲ CISSY HOUSTON, *RIGHT*, HELPED HER DAUGHTER MANAGE HER NEW FAME.

Her growing fame made it harder and harder for Houston to go out in public unnoticed. She could not eat at a restaurant or shop at a mall without attracting the attention of adoring fans. While she appreciated the support, she missed her privacy. As she explained,

I guess it was also this transformation you go through from being totally unknown to being really known. And all these accolades, and all these new people admiring you, calling your name, and you don't even know 'em. It was just a little much for me.[10]

The Greatest Love World Tour

Not long after *Whitney Houston's* release, Houston went on tour with other artists, performing with R&B singers Luther Vandross and Jeffrey Osborne as an opening act. But her fame quickly reached the point where she had a large enough fan base to embark on a concert tour of her own. Her mega-successful 1986 Greatest Love World Tour drew crowds across the United States and in Europe, Japan, and Australia.

She was grateful her voice allowed her to make a living doing what she loved best. Still, like most people, sometimes she just wanted to be left alone.

But no recording artist who hopes to have a lasting career can rest on the success of one album, no matter how well received it may be. Eventually, Houston needed to go back into the studio and make her second album. Could she and Davis keep the momentum going from *Whitney Houston*? Could they impress listeners again?

4

SHE DOES IT AGAIN

The numbers confirmed it: Houston was a pop superstar. With the release of her second album, *Whitney*, on June 2, 1987, she earned the distinction of being the first female artist ever to debut at Number 1 on the *Billboard 200* chart, *Billboard* magazine's weekly ranking of the top-selling albums in the country. *Whitney* held on to this top spot for a record-breaking 11 consecutive weeks.

▶ IN 1987, HOUSTON PERFORMED IN NEW YORK CITY AT MADISON SQUARE GARDEN, ONE OF THE WORLD'S MOST FAMOUS VENUES.

TAKING CRITICISM

Music critics proved harder to please than the general public. Vince Aletti, who reviewed *Whitney* for *Rolling Stone*, said the new songs were "barely distinguishable from Houston's old hits."[1] In his opinion, her latest upbeat dance number, "I Wanna Dance with Somebody (Who Loves Me)," sounded disappointingly similar to "How Will I Know," and the new "Didn't We Almost Have It All" was practically a twin to "The Greatest Love of All." He acknowledged Houston's talent, but thought that by sticking to the same formula of smoothly produced pop songs, Houston was wasting her potential.

Not every critic agreed with Aletti's assessment, however. Richard Corliss of *Time* described this second album as being "bolder, blacker, badder" than the first.[2] Reviewer Dolores Barclay claimed that, despite the risk-free material, "Whitney Houston has a fine

Breaking the Record

Houston's seven consecutive Number 1 hit singles broke the Beatles' and the Bee Gees' previous record of six consecutive Number 1 hits. The seven songs that climbed to the very top of the charts for Houston were, in order of release:

(From her album *Whitney Houston*)
- "Saving All My Love for You"
- "How Will I Know"
- "Greatest Love of All"

(From her album *Whitney*)
- "I Wanna Dance with Somebody (Who Loves Me)"
- "Didn't We Almost Have It All"
- "So Emotional"
- "Where Do Broken Hearts Go"

instrument and uses it well. Her voice takes us to places we know . . . and to places we dream about."[3] And Houston herself spoke out against her reputation as Davis's puppet: "I've always had input . . . in choosing songs, in what the video concept was, in how I looked."[4]

The lighthearted, up-tempo "I Wanna Dance with Somebody (Who Loves Me)" quickly became her most popular song from the album and her fourth consecutive Number 1 single. The song's video features a bouncy, widely smiling Houston searching for just the right dance partner. It was a big hit on MTV—so big the toy company Mattel created a Whitney Houston Barbie doll, sold dressed in a re-creation of one of the many outfits she wears in the video.

However, some people called her a "Barbie" as an insult. In their view, she resembled a plastic doll—too perfect, too smooth, too slickly packaged. And to many African Americans, her perfect plastic image looked too white. Joy Duckett Cain, a reporter for *Essence* magazine,

---

Moment of Truth World Tour

Just a month after the release of *Whitney*, Houston promoted the album by embarking on her second world concert tour, Moment of Truth. She started the tour on July 4, 1987, and, in the next year and a half, performed 90 shows in North America, plus more in Europe, Asia, and Australia. For the US leg of the tour, she traveled with her pet cats, Marilyn and Miste Blu.

summed up Houston's dilemma as a crossover artist in these terms:

> *Perhaps more than any other contemporary superstar, she is in the position of having great mass popularity without eliciting great passion, of being liked but not particularly loved, especially by the Black community. Yeah, we buy her records, but do we buy her act?*[5]

Yet the lukewarm critical reception of her albums had little effect on Houston's soaring commercial success. As *Whitney* racked up sales and awards, including a Grammy and multiple American Music Awards, she rose into the ranks of the entertainment industry's wealthiest performers. *Forbes* magazine placed her at Number 8, one spot above Michael Jackson, on their list of highest-paid entertainers for 1986–1987. She was the list's second-highest ranked female—only Madonna earned more—and the third-highest ranked African American beneath Bill Cosby and Eddie Murphy.

Olympic Tribute

Various musicians and singers contributed songs for television network NBC's coverage of the 1988 Summer Olympic Games held in Seoul, South Korea. Houston's contribution was "One Moment in Time." Its inspirational lyrics are about persevering against the odds. Included on the 1988 Summer Olympics album, the song climbed onto top-ten singles charts around the world.

▲ As part of her work with the Youth Leadership Forum, Houston met with President George H. W. Bush in 1990.

Giving Back

On June 11, 1988, Houston had the honor of joining a large group of performers at London's Wembley Stadium for a six-hour televised concert in celebration of one of her heroes— antiapartheid leader and future South African president Nelson Mandela. At the time, Mandela was still a prisoner of the South African apartheid government, which advocated white supremacy and enforced the segregation of the country's whites and blacks. In Houston's modeling days, she took a stand against apartheid by refusing to allow her photos to appear in South African magazines. Later, she turned down invitations to give concerts in South Africa. Mandela's wife Winnie sent Houston a thank-you note praising the singer's actions. "For a long time both I and my children have admired you and have always known that you do care," Winnie wrote.[6] Cissy said that awareness of social issues was a top priority for Houston. "She [has] raised a whole lot of money for different charities. She does it because she wants to. She loves it. She wants to be some kind of help to her people," Cissy explained to a reporter for *JET* magazine.[7]

Houston's charity work was far reaching. She wanted to get married and start a family someday, but she was not ready to give her mother grandchildren just yet. Instead, in 1989, she entrusted her mother with the newly created Whitney Houston Foundation for Children. The charitable organization worked to raise funds for children facing a variety of hardships, such as homelessness, acquired immunodeficiency syndrome (AIDS), cancer, and illiteracy.

MEETING BOBBY

Houston's hectic career left her little time for a personal life. In 1987, she had purchased a large house in suburban Mendham, New Jersey, but with long intervals on the road touring and promoting her album, she barely lived there. Her schedule left little room for romance. She dated actor Eddie Murphy and NFL quarterback Randall Cunningham, but neither relationship lasted. She told her mother she wanted to "grab for the simple things in life"—to have a husband and kids.[8] Cissy advised her to be patient.

Then, at the 1989 Soul Train Awards ceremony, she bumped into R&B singer Bobby Brown—literally. As Houston remembered that

Whitney's House

As Houston told reporter David Van Biema in *Life* magazine, it took a while for her to feel comfortable in the 20,000 square-foot (1,858 sq m) ranch home she purchased in Mendham, New Jersey, in 1987. The house featured a recording studio in the basement and a backyard swimming pool with her initials spelled in 16-foot (5 m) black Plexiglas letters at the bottom. As Houston explained,

I designed [the house] on the road—picked out the blinds— but here I was moved in, and it was like it wasn't mine. The bedroom was so large, sometimes it seemed like it was swallowing me. And I'd sleep in the maid's quarters. People used to laugh at me, but I needed to get a grasp on it, you know, my living space.[9]

At the time, the singer owned an additional home in North Miami Beach, Florida.

The Soul Train Awards

Soul Train was a televised dance show that aired from 1970 to 2006 and spotlighted primarily African-American music, including R&B, hip-hop, and soul. In 1987, the show's producers began hosting an award ceremony honoring African-American recording artists. Since that year, the awards have been given annually. Winners at the Soul Train Awards receive statuettes in the shape of African ceremonial masks.

night, she sat in the row behind Brown in the theater and kept accidentally jostling him while she laughed and joked with her friends. She apologized and he responded sternly, "Yeah, well, just don't let it happen again." Instead of being put off by his abrupt manner, she was intrigued: "Well, I always get curious when somebody doesn't like me. I want to know why. So I said, 'I'm going to invite Bobby to a party.' And I did."[10] Much to her surprise, he accepted her invitation. And when she saw him again a few months later at a mutual friend's party, he asked her on a date.

Immediately, Houston felt comfortable around Brown. "He was the first male I met in the business that I could talk to and be real with," she explained.[11] Houston was famous for singing about love, and she was now finally finding love for herself.

▲ IT WAS ALMOST LOVE AT FIRST SIGHT FOR HOUSTON
AND BROWN.

5

A NEW LOVE

hrough the media, word spread that Houston and Brown were dating, and immediately questions arose. Many wondered whether the two singers had genuine feelings for each other or if their relationship was just a publicity stunt. Was America's pop princess trying to give herself an edge by associating with a notorious "bad boy" of R&B? Was Brown hoping his girlfriend's squeaky-clean image would wipe away rumors about his hard-partying lifestyle?

▶ IN THE EARLY 1990S, HOUSTON BEGAN SHOWING AN EDGIER SIDE OF HERSELF.

Or maybe the media's portrayal of Houston and Brown had never reflected their true personalities. As Houston explained to reporter Anthony Curtis in *Rolling Stone*, while a person's image is "part of [the person], it's not the whole picture. I am not always in a sequined gown. I am nobody's angel."[1]

BROWN'S BACKGROUND

A closer look at Houston's and Brown's backgrounds revealed similarities and differences. "You know, Bobby and I basically come from the same place," Houston said in *Rolling Stone*. "Bobby comes from Boston, out of the projects. I come from Newark out of the projects."[2]

However, Whitney's childhood suburb of East Orange was middle class, in contrast to the rough, impoverished Roxbury section of Boston where Brown grew up. Brown realized early on he needed to work hard to escape the gang violence that took the lives of many young African-American men in his neighborhood. At age 11, after a friend was stabbed

The Projects

Public housing projects, informally known as the projects, are government-subsidized apartment buildings or single-family homes rented at reduced rates to people living at or below the poverty level. Though most residents are law abiding, the projects have a reputation for higher levels of gang violence and other criminal activity. Technically, Houston never lived in the projects.

to death, Brown reevaluated his priorities and became determined to have a career in music. His older brother Tommy described Bobby's transformation this way:

> *As kids, everyone had their dreams, but his loss made him more determined. He started getting serious about music the way other kids in Roxbury might get serious about playing pro basketball.*[3]

Both Houston and Brown began singing in church. Both received offers from record companies in their early teens. Brown was 12 years old when he and four of his friends formed the band New Edition. He was 14 when producer and talent scout Maurice Starr discovered the band performing in his Boston-area talent show and subsequently landed them a contract with a small recording company, Streetwise Records. Based on the success of New Edition's 1983 album with Streetwise, *CandyGirl*, MCA Records took on the group and produced their even more popular second album, *New Edition.* Reviewers compared the group's effervescent pop style to that of the Jackson 5, and they compared Brown to a young Michael Jackson.

In 1985, Brown left New Edition to pursue a solo career. His 1988 breakout album, *Don't*

Be Cruel, established him as one of the leaders in the New Jack Swing style of music, which was a blend of hip-hop, dance pop, and R&B that appeared in the late 1980s and early 1990s.

CHANGES AND NEW CHALLENGES

Watching her boyfriend in concert, Houston admired his dynamic stage presence. "Bobby's very sensual. . . . Women watch [him] with an intensity that I've never seen before," she told an interviewer.[4] His dance moves proved too sensual for police in Columbus, Georgia, who arrested him for inappropriate behavior during a 1989 show. A judge sentenced Brown to pay a fine of $600. But Houston felt inspired by Brown's unrestrained attitude, admitting, "I've learned to be freer with Bobby. I've learned to be a little more loose. Not so contained, you know?"[5]

It had been three years since *Whitney*'s release. From Houston's perspective, the relatively long break had been necessary for her and her fans. "I think the public had about enough of me," she told Tom Green of *USA Today*, "and I had

▲ BROWN WAS A HIGHLY SUCCESSFUL SOLO ARTIST BY THE LATE 1980S.

enough of me, too." She had cut back on touring and performing in favor of spending time at home, saying she did so "just to get to know me again."[6]

When Houston went back into the studio to record her next album, she followed Brown's lead and hired two producers who had played a major part in shaping *Don't Be Cruel* into the best-selling R&B album of 1988. Antonio "L. A." Reid and Babyface (born Kenneth Edmonds) had produced records and written music for some of the industry's hottest artists. Houston knew they could give her music the funky, urban groove critics felt she had been lacking. Her third album, *I'm Your Baby Tonight*, released in November 1990 to mixed reviews but commercial success.

With more time to catch her breath and think, Houston decided she wanted to take on a new challenge—one she had previously avoided. In 1990,

A New Side of Houston

I'm Your Baby Tonight, Houston's third studio album, was different from her previous two. Judging from the cover photo of her sitting sideways on a motorcycle with a license plate that reads "Nippy" and city lights glowing behind her, listeners were supposed to find a tougher, more streetwise singer with a grittier, less polished message—what many of her critics said they had wanted all along. Yet, once again, reactions were mixed. *Rolling Stone* reviewer James Hunter declared it "her best and most integrated album," meaning all the songs fit together well.[7] However, David Browne, writing in *Entertainment Weekly*, called the new material "relentlessly superficial—and proud of it" and gave the album the near-failing grade of D+.[8] Nonetheless, *I'm Your Baby Tonight* reached Number 1 on *Billboard*'s R&B/Hip-Hop chart and Number 3 on the *Billboard 200*. It also spawned two Number 1 hit singles—the title track "I'm Your Baby Tonight" and "All the Man That I Need."

after years of turning down movie roles, she accepted a part that seemed perfect for her. She agreed to play Rachel Marron, a pop singer receiving death threats from an obsessed fan, in the Hollywood motion picture *The Bodyguard*. As a pop star, Houston's voice had resounded through radios and stereos for the last half of the 1980s. It was a new decade, and it was time for Houston to light up the big screen as a movie star.

"After I met her, my whole outlook on a lot of things changed. I think I was with the wrong people to understand what love was about. They didn't understand me . . . they never trusted me. They were wondering what I was doing on the road or somewhere. [Whitney] gives me that freedom to be myself."[9]
—*Brown describing his relationship with Houston in 1992*

6

A Big Role, A Big Song, A Big Day

ouston loved movies, especially classics featuring her favorite actors—Paul Robeson, Dorothy Dandridge, Greta Garbo, and Lauren Bacall. But the thought of acting in a movie herself initially filled her with dread. How could she not feel scared when she, a rookie, would be acting alongside Kevin Costner, one of Hollywood's most accomplished and attractive leading men?

It took her two years to work up the courage to tell Costner she would take the role.

▲ Houston with Costner in a scene from *The Bodyguard*

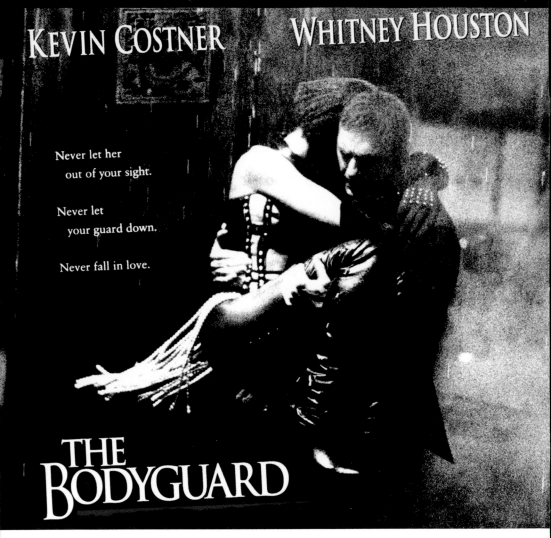

KEVIN COSTNER   WHITNEY HOUSTON

Never let her
out of your sight.

Never let
your guard down.

Never fall in love.

THE
BODYGUARD

▲ MOVIE POSTER FROM *THE BODYGUARD*

In addition to playing bodyguard Frank Farmer,
Costner was also one of the film's producers, and
he did not want to make the movie without her.
As Costner explained, "There are certain singers

that occupy that territory that includes a world-class voice, real elegance, and a physical presence. Diana Ross and Barbra Streisand are two. Whitney Houston is one."[1]

However, he finally got tired of waiting for her to decide and called her on the phone, demanding an answer. She remembered telling him honestly, "I'm afraid. I don't want to go out there and fail."[2] He assured her she would not— he would not let her. He also told her not to take acting lessons. He wanted her to appear fresh and natural on screen.

MAKING THE BODYGUARD

Filming began in the fall of 1991. In the story, pop star Rachel Marron's manager hires Frank Farmer, a former Secret Service agent, to protect her from a stalker. Houston had never required heavy security. Still, her celebrity lifestyle mirrored her character's in many respects. However, she could not just coast through the role. She worked hard to give a convincing performance.

The Movie Poster Controversy

The official movie poster for *The Bodyguard* features a photo of Farmer carrying Marron away from danger. Her head is bent against his shoulder, and some people accused the film company, Warner Bros. Pictures, of choosing this pose specifically to hide Houston's dark skin. Houston dismissed the rumor, saying, "I mean, people know who Whitney Houston is—you can't hide the fact that I'm black."[3]

Houston said her hardest scene was a highly dramatic one in which Marron and Farmer argue, and Marron ends up slapping him. She remembered thinking during filming, "Oh, God, I don't wanna hit this man 'cause this man didn't do anything to me. And I had to really slap him hard."[4] But, thanks to Costner's patient coaching, she got through it. Ultimately, Houston and Costner became good friends, and she paid him back for all the acting lessons by giving him singing lessons.

At least one part of working on *The Bodyguard* was familiar to Houston: recording songs for the movie's soundtrack.

Kevin Costner

Actor Kevin Costner first broke into show business by playing a corpse. In the 1983 blockbuster movie *The Big Chill,* his character Alex commits suicide. However, all his scenes were later cut, with the exception of the opening shot of the mortician dressing Alex's body for the funeral. Costner went on to more prominent roles in the cowboy buddy movie *Silverado* (1985), the classic baseball comedy *Bull Durham* (1988), and the Civil War–era epic *Dances With Wolves* (1990), which he not only starred in but also directed. *Dances With Wolves* won seven Academy Awards, including Best Picture and Best Director. Not long after *The Bodyguard*, Costner achieved dubious fame for codirecting and starring in *Waterworld* (1995). At the time, the film was one of the most expensive Hollywood flops ever. More than a decade later, in 2007, his singing lessons with Houston finally paid off, and he founded his own country rock band, Kevin Costner and Modern West. The band released three albums between 2008 and 2011.

▲ HOUSTON PERFORMING AS MARRON IN
THE BODYGUARD

Her mother often accompanied her to the film
set, and Cissy clearly remembered the day her
daughter recorded one particular number, "I Will

Second Choice

"I Will Always Love You" was not the first choice of song for the movie. The filmmakers had planned for Houston to sing "What Becomes of the Bro- kenhearted," but they discovered it was already being used in another movie, *Fried Green Toma- toes,* scheduled for release later that year. At the last minute, Costner found "I Will Always Love You" and thought Houston could give it her own soulful spin. And he was right.

Always Love You." Written and first performed in the 1970s by country singer Dolly Parton, the song plays during the movie's romantic final scene, when Farmer kisses Marron good-bye at the airport. On set, Cissy had a profound emotional response to it:

> *From the control room, I watched her sing "I Will Always Love You" and wept. The song summed up everything I felt for my daughter. . . . When she emerged from the studio to listen to playback, I told her the song was going to be a huge hit. "You think so, Ma?" she asked.*[5]

THE WEDDING

The movie would not be released for another year, which meant they had to wait and see if Cissy's prediction would come true. In the meantime, Houston had a wedding to plan.

On July 18, 1992, in a gazebo decorated with thousands of lavender and purple roses, Houston and Brown were married on the grounds of her

New Jersey estate before a crowd of 800 family members and friends. The bride was almost 29 years old; the groom was 23.

For Cissy, the event was bittersweet. Although she approved of her daughter's choice of a husband, Cissy had recently gone through an unwelcome change in her own life. Her husband John had filed for divorce after 35 years of marriage. She did not want to see him at the wedding, nor did she enjoy thinking about the distance Houston's new commitment would likely put between mother and daughter.

Though Cissy's married life was ending, Houston's was just beginning. Now Houston really did seem to have it all—a phenomenally successful career and a fulfilling personal life. No wonder journalist Anne Trebbe, who interviewed the singer for *USA Today* not long before the wedding, remarked, "Whitney Houston is a princess in a seemingly perfect fairy tale."[6]

Purple Day

Houston incorporated her favorite color, purple, into practically every aspect of her wedding decor. The bridesmaids wore purple gowns, the groomsmen wore purple tuxedos and purple shoes, and purple fabric lined the tents at the reception. Additionally, thousands of purple flowers, mostly roses and orchids, adorned the grounds. Anything that was not purple was either lavender or white.

The Honeymoon

Houston and Brown planned a honeymoon trip that was just as lavish as their wedding ceremony and reception. They jetted to Europe and then boarded a luxury yacht for a ten-day cruise of the French Riviera. The vacation was a gift from their record companies, Arista and MCA, and it was one of the only wedding presents they kept for themselves. They had asked wedding guests not to buy them gifts but instead to donate money to the Whitney Houston Foundation for Children.

Yes, Houston had her prince, but there was still one piece needed to complete her vision of happily ever after. She wanted a baby.

———•◆•———

▲ HOUSTON AND BROWN HAD A FAIRY-TALE WEDDING.

7

BEHIND THE MASK

"Here, at last, is a princess fantasy to make Cinderella jealous," wrote *Entertainment Weekly* movie critic Owen Gleiberman in his December 4, 1992, review of *The Bodyguard*. The remark was not intended as a compliment. In his opinion, the movie was all shiny surface and no substance, and its female star seemed, much like a fairy-tale princess, too good to be true. He compared Houston to "a diamond without flaws" and called her beauty a mask beneath which "one never senses a glimmer of vulnerability, pain,

▶ HOUSTON AND COSTNER ATTENDED *THE BODYGUARD* PREMIER ON NOVEMBER 23, 1992.

doubt."[1] Gleiberman's comments echoed the criticism her music often received.

New York Times newspaper reviewer Janet Maslin criticized the on-screen romance between Houston's and Costner's characters. Maslin felt they lacked chemistry together and relied on "the swelling of the hit-bound soundtrack to suggest any passion."[2]

Other reviewers praised her debut. Roger Ebert of the *Chicago Sun-Times* said, "She photographs wonderfully and has a warm smile, and yet is able to suggest selfish and egotistical dimensions in the character."[3]

Moviegoers flocked to the theaters, making *The Bodyguard* the seventh-highest earning film of 1992. The soundtrack went on to become the best-selling soundtrack of all time, with Houston's "I Will Always Love You" ultimately selling more copies than any other single by a female singer. Looking back over Houston's career, many people believe her

"And one day I was riding along in the car and had just turned the radio on, and I heard her start that a capella, like 'If I should stay.' And it took me a few seconds, and I thought, 'What is that? That's so familiar.' And then when she went into, you know, like the 'I Will Always Love You,' I just about had a heart attack and died. I just about wrecked. It was a great feeling, though. What a great record she did on that."[4]
—*Dolly Parton remembering the first time she heard Houston sing "I Will Always Love You," 2003*

version of this song and her 1991 "Star-Spangled Banner" are her greatest achievements.

BECOMING A MOTHER

As 1992 came to a close, Houston cared more about an upcoming event in her personal life than her professional success. She was going to have a baby. As she told a reporter for *Entertainment Weekly*, her anticipation of motherhood sometimes made her career seem distant, like it belonged to somebody else. As she put it,

> *It's so weird watching [the media] talk about The Bodyguard. . . . I mean, I'm lying in bed, holding my stomach, watching my baby move, and they're talking about 'the Bodyguard phenomenon.' I just feel far removed from it, like it's déjà vu.*[5]

On March 5, 1993, Bobbi Kristina Houston-Brown was born. Brown already had three children from previous relationships, but Bobbi Kristina—called Bobbi Kris or Krissy—would be Houston's only child. Houston welcomed her daughter with the same level of joy and intensity her own parents had felt at her birth. "I never thought I could love anyone as much as I love her," she gushed to an interviewer.[6]

As Houston's passion for her daughter and husband grew, her passion for her career began to fade. She confessed to *Rolling Stone*'s Anthony DeCurtis that because she had been working for more than half her life—modeling, performing in clubs, recording, touring—she already felt old at age 29. She wanted to stay home with her family instead of jumping back into the high-stress, fast-paced world of pop superstardom.

DEALING WITH FAME

Yet stepping out of the spotlight at this point was nearly impossible. The movie's soundtrack in particular had taken off, continuing to sell steadily and winning practically every award it was nominated for, including the 1993 Grammy for Album of the Year. Houston won two additional Grammys that year, Record of the Year and Best Pop Vocal Performance, Female. Houston had little choice but to hold on and go along for the ride. After *The Bodyguard*, Houston appeared in a string of successful movies throughout the 1990s.

▲ HOUSTON WITH BABY BOBBI, 1993

Brown told his wife he would support her however he could. If she needed to tour and travel to promote the album, he would put his own career on hold to be by her side. Brown may have felt some jealousy because of his wife's

denzel
WASHINGTON

whitney
HOUSTON

They needed help.

What they got was a miracle.

The
Preacher's
Wife

▲ *THE PREACHER'S WIFE* WAS ONE OF HOUSTON'S
SUCCESSFUL MOVIES IN THE 1990S.

fame. His 1992 album *Bobby* sold more than 1 million copies, but it did not do nearly as well commercially as *Don't Be Cruel*. He wanted to be known as an R&B star, not as Mr. Whitney Houston, but her career was overshadowing his.

The tabloid newspapers had begun reporting gossip about the couple's marriage practically as soon as their wedding ceremony ended. They said Brown drank excessively, did drugs, and partied with other women. Houston defended her husband. Just because Brown had the image of a bad boy did not mean he was one in real life. She claimed,

> *People don't know Bobby because there hasn't been much on Bobby except that Bobby is this sexy man who does all this bumping and grinding. But Bobby is a family man. Bobby loves his mother, loves his family. . . . I know where my husband is; I know what my husband does.*[7]

Busy with her movie career,

Movie Roles

Through the second half of the 1990s, Houston was busy making movies. In 1995, she costarred in *Waiting to Exhale*, a film about four African-American female friends and the ups and downs of their relationships with men. She played the title role in the 1996 Christmas movie *The Preacher's Wife*, starring alongside Oscar-winning actor Denzel Washington. Cissy appeared alongside her daughter as Mrs. Havergal, a member of the church choir. Houston's character, Julia, was the choir director. Houston also sang on the successful soundtrack albums for the two films.

Through her own production company, Brownhouse Productions, Houston launched a televised remake of the classic musical *Cinderella* in 1997. Popular R&B singer Brandy starred as the rags-to-riches fairy-tale heroine. Houston played the role of Cinderella's fairy godmother.

> "My hope for Bobbi Kris is for her to always be true to herself, no matter what people might say or think. You have to do what you feel is right, what you know is right. Be true to yourself. Be a decent human being."[10]
> —Houston speaking of her daughter, 1995

Houston did not release another studio album until 1998's *My Love Is Your Love*. It was no match for the record-breaking sales numbers of her first two albums; still, *My Love Is Your Love* gave her some of the best reviews she had ever received. A writer from *The Village Voice* repeated what many others in the media were saying when he called it her "sharpest and most satisfying album so far."[8]

ART REFLECTS LIFE?

Right before the album's release, Houston admitted in *Billboard* magazine that she was no longer interested in singing starry-eyed ballads:

> *I wasn't into the syrupy kind of vibe. I just didn't feel like singing "I Will Always Love You." I'm a working mother, I'm a wife, I'm an artist. There are so many things that go into that, and it's not always like "Everything is beautiful in its own way."*[9]

Now, instead of the soaring romanticism of "The Greatest Love of All," listeners found an edgy realism in the new album's first track,

"It's Not Right But It's Okay," about a woman surviving a failed relationship. The album also features the feisty, fed-up "In My Business," a song presumed to address the tabloid scrutiny of Houston's own marriage.

It began to seem as if the scrutiny was merited. In October 1998, Brown spent five days in jail in Broward County, Florida, after being sentenced for a January incident of driving under the influence of alcohol. When he showed up drunk to serve his sentence, a judge ordered him to enter a drug and alcohol rehabilitation program after he got out of jail. While his wife made appearances to promote her new album, Brown underwent 30 days of inpatient treatment in a clinic in Minnesota.

Contrary to what the song said, maybe things were not right. Maybe they were not even okay. Reports would soon surface that Brown was not doing drugs alone. His wife had been doing drugs with him.

———•◆•———

8

FALLING STAR

Because *My Love Is Your Love* was a different kind of Houston album, more intimate and personal than its predecessors, the singer wanted its concert tour to be different as well. Instead of performing in massive arenas for 20,000 fans per night, she purposely booked shows in venues with less than half that number of seats. As Houston told the press, "This is about playing places where people can actually feel you, can actually know what you're wearing, what clothes you have on."[1]

▶ HOUSTON OPENED HER MY LOVE IS YOUR LOVE TOUR IN CHICAGO.

On June 22, 1999, the first night of the tour, Houston took the stage at Chicago's Arie Crown Theater, changing outfits several times throughout the evening to show off the fashionable wardrobe designers Dolce & Gabbana had provided for her. Six-year-old Bobbi Kristina came out to sing with her mom for one number.

However, fans in five other US cities were not as lucky as the fans in Chicago. Claiming throat problems brought on by bronchitis, Houston pulled out of shows at the last minute in her hometown of Newark; Washington DC; Memphis, Tennessee; Saint Louis, Missouri; and San Francisco, California. In San Francisco, she canceled the show 15 minutes before it was supposed to start. News

"When You Believe"

One of the tracks on *My Love Is Your Love* is a duet sung by Houston and another powerhouse vocalist, Mariah Carey. The two singers, who were previously reported to be rivals, originally recorded "When You Believe" for the 1998 DreamWorks animated film *The Prince of Egypt*, a biblical story based on the life of Moses. Carey included the song on her own album, *#1s*. Carey told MTV News how she and Houston first became interested in collaborating. "Actually, Jeffrey Katzenberg from DreamWorks showed us both the movie separately and got us both excited about the project." She downplayed the talk of "diva-ism" during the recording process and, referring to Houston, said, "She was just really cool, and we had a really good time in the studio."[2] "When You Believe" won the Oscar for Best Original Song at the seventy-first Academy Awards ceremony.

▲ HOUSTON AND BROWN ATTENDED A PARTY BEFORE THE 2000 GRAMMYS. FANS BEGAN WORRYING THE SINGERS WERE ABUSING DRUGS.

stories suggested a darker explanation for the cancellations: substance abuse.

INCREASING TROUBLES

Other than vague reports of odd backstage behavior, no evidence for this claim surfaced until the January 11, 2000, incident in Hawaii, when airport security found marijuana in Houston's bag. Two months after that, she failed to show up for a performance at the ceremony to induct her mentor Davis into the Rock and Roll Hall of Fame. Then she was cut from the 2000 Academy Awards ceremony for reportedly messing up during rehearsals. Scheduled to sing "Over the Rainbow," she apparently could not get the words right. Observers said Houston acted jittery and unfocused and started singing the wrong song. Around that same time she arrived four hours late for a photo shoot with *Jane* magazine. When she finally did show up, Houston could barely keep her eyes open and played an imaginary piano. Houston blamed the fiasco on having gone to the dentist earlier in the day to have a cracked tooth repaired.

Back in 1991, Houston had talked with Lynn Norment of *Ebony* about the high price of fame. "You wake up every day with a magnifying glass over you," she said. "Somebody,

Not under Arrest

After word got out about the incident in Hawaii, some people wondered why airport security allowed Houston and Brown to board their flight instead of taking them into custody. According to reports, officers seized Houston's bag and called police, but, since airport security personnel are not officially police officers, they do not have the authority to make arrests. The flight left with Houston and Brown on it before the police arrived.

somewhere is speaking your name every five seconds of the day, whether it's positive or negative."[3] Throughout the late 1980s and early 1990s, the image in the magnifying glass had been that of a gorgeous, rich, hardworking superstar with an incomparable voice. Houston seemed to live the perfect life. In reality, she did not. As she also told Norment in the interview, everybody has problems, and "problems don't change, no matter if you have millions, billions or zillions [of dollars]."[4]

Almost ten years later, reports of Houston's problems clouded news of her recent accomplishments. She released her *Whitney Houston: The Greatest Hits* album in May 2000, and it rose as high as Number 5 on the pop charts. In August 2001, she signed an incredible new contract with Arista, the biggest-ever deal in the record company's history. They agreed to pay her more than $100 million to produce six albums in the coming years.

A Break with Davis

In 2000, BMG, the parent company of Arista Records, removed Davis from Arista and replaced him with producer L. A. Reid. BMG then appointed Davis to head a new label, J Records, where he discovered stars such as Alicia Keys. Houston stayed with Arista, but she did not relish the idea of being without her mentor. As she explained, "Clive was my man for all those years. Where was I going? It frightened me. It frightens me."[5]

▲ HOUSTON'S APPEARANCE AND PERFORMANCE AT
A MICHAEL JACKSON TRIBUTE CONCERT LEFT FANS
WORRYING ABOUT HER HEALTH.

None of her successes stopped fans from
worrying—and the media from gossiping—
when, in 2001, she appeared alarmingly thin on
a televised tribute to her friend Michael Jackson.

Rumors spread that she was dying or that she was already dead. She issued a statement reassuring everyone that she was still very much alive. Yet it seemed obvious from her skeletal frame that something was seriously wrong. People speculated that she had an eating disorder or was wasting away from drug abuse.

"Emotionally, he was abusive. Physically, no way. Because first of all, I was raised with two boys. I will fight you back. I will fight you back with anything I can find."[6]

—*Houston on rumors of Brown's abuse, 2009*

THE INTERVIEW

A few weeks before the release of Houston's fifth studio album *Just Whitney*, she appeared in a much-publicized 2002 television interview. At Houston and Brown's new house in Atlanta, Georgia, ABC newscaster Diane Sawyer candidly asked tough questions. She conversed with the couple about their marriage. They denied stories that Brown had physically abused his wife. Houston claimed she was more likely to hit Brown during an argument than the other way around.

Sawyer addressed Houston's recent history of cancellations, missed appearances, and strange behavior. Houston partly attributed it to stress, but she did not deny having past experience with drugs. When Sawyer asked her to name which drug—"Is it alcohol? Is it marijuana? Is it cocaine? Is it pills?"—Houston answered softly, "It has been. At times."[7] But the segment of the interview most often quoted in follow-up news stories was Houston's vehement assertion that she had never, and would never, smoke the highly addictive form of cocaine known as crack because, in her words, "crack is cheap. I make too much money to ever smoke crack. Let's get that straight. OK? We don't do crack. We don't do that. Crack is whack."[8]

Sawyer ended the interview by asking, "Ten years from now, give me the perfect life for Whitney Houston." Houston responded, "Retired. Sitting, looking at my daughter grow up, become a great woman of God, grandchildren."[9] For this vision of the future to come true, Houston would have to stop her abuse of drugs and alcohol. And she would have to tangle with what she had identified to Sawyer as "the biggest devil"[10] of them all: herself. As she explained in the interview,

"Crack Is Whack"

Houston got this saying from a mural that artist Keith Haring painted without permission in a New York City playground in 1986. Haring died of AIDS in 1990, but his mural still exists. The city parks department restored it and changed the name of the area where it stands, on the wall of a handball court, to the Crack Is Whack Playground.

▲ DIANE SAWYER ASKED HOUSTON MANY PERSONAL
QUESTIONS DURING THEIR 2002 INTERVIEW.

*Nobody makes me do anything I don't want to
do. It's my decision. So the biggest devil is me.
I'm either my best friend or my worst enemy.
And that's how I have to deal with it.[11]*

9

ONE DAY AT A TIME

ouston had ruined her voice. That was what everybody was saying, anyway. It was the spring of 2010, and she had just begun the European stretch of her Nothing But Love tour, her first concert tour in more than ten years. Fans flocked to her shows, but once there, many complained about what they heard and saw. A concertgoer in Birmingham, England, described Houston's performance: "She was rasping and rambling. She couldn't sing, it was horrendous and I shall be asking for my money back."[1] In Birmingham and

▸ HOUSTON'S PERFORMANCES DURING HER 2010 EUROPEAN TOUR WERE WIDELY CRITICIZED.

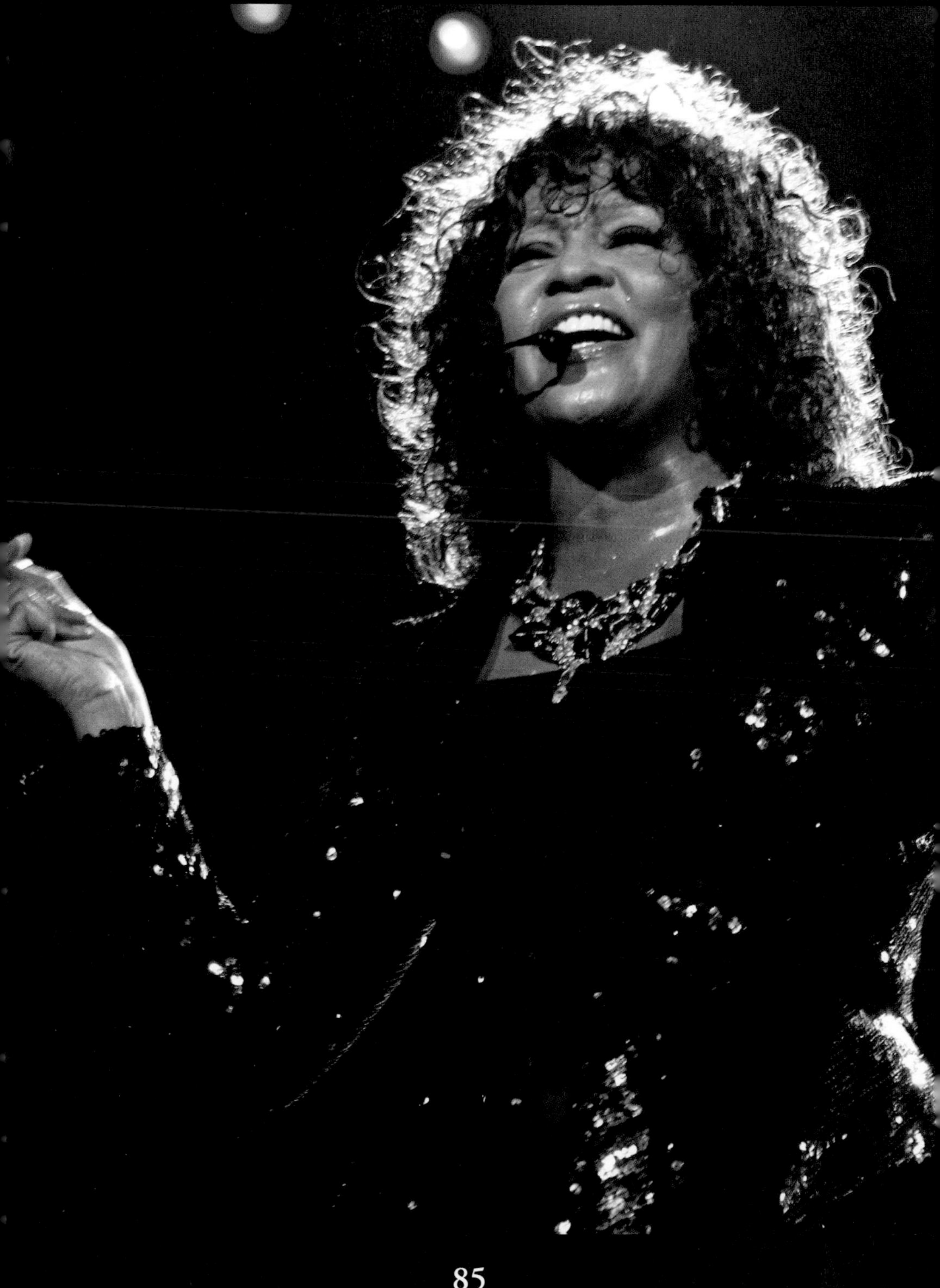

at tour stops in Australia, some members of the audience booed. Others left early in disgust.

As singers age, they often lose vocal power and finesse. At 46, Houston understandably no longer had the pipes of the 22-year-old who trilled up and down the musical scale with ease on *Whitney Houston.* But listening to her struggle to perform her old hits and new songs from 2009's *I Look to You*, her first studio album in seven years, people suspected more than the usual wear and tear. They believed her years of admitted drug use worsened her decline.

Reunited with Her Mentor

I Look to You marked a return to Houston's collaboration with her friend and mentor Davis. She had been mostly absent from the music scene since her 2002 album *Just Whitney,* until Davis called Houston and told her, "It's time for you to come back and sing for us again."[2] Released in August 2009, the album generated two singles—"I Look to You" and "Million Dollar Bill"—that reached the top 20 on *Billboard*'s R&B/Hip-Hop chart.

THE OPRAH INTERVIEW

A few months before, in September 2009, Houston sat down with Oprah Winfrey for a candid interview in which she described how low her addiction had taken her. Houston told the talk show host that by the mid-1990s, she was doing drugs such as cocaine and marijuana every day. She described sitting on the couch with Brown for weeklong stretches, just watching television and getting high. It got so bad, Houston said, that at one point her mother showed up with the sheriff. They were ready to drag her to jail if she did not agree to go into treatment and get sober. Houston remembered Cissy telling her,

I want my daughter back. . . . I want to see that glow in your eyes. That light in your eyes. I want to see the child I raised. And you weren't raised like this. And I'm not having it.[3]

Those dark days were behind her now, Houston said in the *Oprah* interview. She and Brown had separated in 2006 and divorced in 2007. Though she did not blame Brown completely for her decision to use drugs, she knew they had stayed together longer than they

---

"The Voice"

Winfrey dubbed Houston "The Voice" and said she believes Houston's talent was a gift. In the 2009 interview, Winfrey asked Houston how she could have mistreated her voice and forgotten that it was a gift. Houston responded,

I knew in the days when I was a teenager singing for God. I was so sure. When I became "Whitney Houston" and all this other stuff that happened, my life became the world's. My privacy. My business. Who I was with. Who I married. And I was, like, that's not fair. . . . I just wanted to be normal.[4]

Houston did seek treatment for addiction multiple times. In March 2004, she checked into a drug rehabilitation clinic, but she checked out after five days to continue treatment with a private caregiver. She entered a rehab center again in 2005.

should have—long after their relationship had gone sour—partly to show detractors that their commitment to one another was real.

Houston still had the strength and love of family and friends supporting her. She and Bobbi Kristina, now in her teens and aspiring toward a music career of her own, lived together in Los Angeles. Houston credited her daughter and her Christian faith for giving her the courage to rebuild her life and keep singing. However, she admitted to Oprah that the temptation to use drugs would probably always be there.

THE LAST PROJECT

In the fall of 2011, Houston's talent was reportedly back in full force on the set of the movie *Sparkle,* a remake of a 1976 film based on the story of legendary group the Supremes. Houston played the disgruntled mother of three singing sisters, with *American Idol* winner Jordin Sparks in the lead role. Houston also recorded songs for the soundtrack. Bishop T. D. Jakes, one of the film's producers, noted none of the

A Disastrous Reality Television Show

In 2004, Brown convinced his wife to appear with him in a reality television show called *Being Bobby Brown*, which was filmed at their Atlanta mansion and broadcast for a single season in 2005 on the Bravo network. The show received high ratings, allowing viewers a glimpse into the ugly world of the couple's dysfunctional homelife.

▲ HOUSTON WORKED ON THE MOVIE *SPARKLE* WITH
JORDIN SPARKS DURING THE LAST MONTHS OF HER LIFE.

problems with Houston's voice that concertgoers
griped about in 2010: "When she (Houston)
walked out there to perform, we were all just
stunned at how well she did, not only with the
singing but also with the acting as well."[5] Jakes
predicted the movie's release in August 2012
would revitalize Houston's career.

Instead, the movie would partly be a poignant reminder of a tragic loss. On February 11, 2012, while preparing to appear at Davis's annual pre-Grammy party, Houston died in her room at the Beverly Hilton hotel in Los Angeles. An assistant found her body submerged in the bathtub at approximately 3:35 p.m. Paramedics arrived approximately ten minutes later and tried unsuccessfully to revive the singer before pronouncing her dead at 3:55 p.m. She was 48 years old.

A HOME-GOING

On the morning of February 18, 2012, a thick cluster of Mylar balloons tied to a wrought-iron fence bobbed in the breeze outside New Hope Baptist Church in Newark. In the days since Houston's death, her fans had left the balloons there as a memorial along with stuffed animals and cardboard signs decorated with photos of Houston.

On the day of Houston's funeral, Newark police cordoned off a six-block radius around the church and encouraged the public to stay home and watch the service on television. Nevertheless, crowds gathered as close to the church as they could to watch the golden hearse with a calligraphy *W* on the back window wend its way

▲ FANS WATCHED HOUSTON'S FUNERAL PROCESSION FROM A DISTANCE.

down Newark's MLK Boulevard toward New Hope. The *W* stood for Whigham Funeral Home, but on that day it also stood for Whitney.

In the Southern Baptist tradition, the service would not be a somber, quiet affair. There would be tears, of course, but there would also be laughter, shouts, and cries of affirmation at this "home-going," a term reflecting the Baptist belief that God had called Houston home to Heaven. One by one, friends got up before the packed church to speak about Houston and celebrate her life.

Costner remembered how much Houston had doubted her acting ability before her screen test for *The Bodyguard* and how she had confessed to him that she worried she would not be good enough. He looked down from the podium at his friend's silver coffin and said, "You weren't just good enough, you were great."[6]

Davis began his eulogy talking about Houston as a professional singer: "Without knowing of her love for music, her passion for music, and her absolute genius for interpreting songs, you really don't know Whitney Houston." But then he moved on to talking about her as a friend. He said, "Personally, all I can say is that I loved her very much."[7]

Dionne Warwick, filmmaker Tyler Perry, Newark mayor Cory Booker, and others spoke about Houston during the funeral, and singers such as Alicia Keys, Stevie Wonder, and R. Kelly performed musical tributes. The service had been scheduled to last two hours. Instead, it lasted four. And even that was not long enough to fully capture the impact Houston had had on the world of pop music and on the many people who had known and loved her personally or simply through hearing her music.

A SAD ENDING

According to the Los Angeles County coroner's office, an autopsy report revealed Houston died of drowning, with symptoms of heart disease. The autopsy also revealed a hole inside Houston's nose that indicated long-term cocaine use. Cocaine, marijuana, and several prescription drugs were in her system at the time of her death.

Yet, the sad end to her life did not negate everything she had accomplished over the course of her career. Not only had she achieved professional success for herself but she had also paved the way for countless female vocalists who came after her. Pop singing sensation Beyoncé

▲ FANS AROUND THE WORLD LEFT TRIBUTES TO HOUSTON
SIMILAR TO THIS ONE LEFT OUTSIDE THE HOTEL WHERE
HOUSTON DIED.

wrote on her Web site the day after Houston's
death,

> I, like every singer, always wanted to be just
> like her. Her voice was perfect. Strong but
> soothing. Soulful and classic. Her vibrato,
> her cadence, her control. So many of my life's
> memories are attached to a Whitney Houston
> song. She is our queen and she opened doors
> and provided a blueprint for all of us.[9]

At the end of the funeral, as the six pallbearers lifted the casket to carry it from the church, a recording of Houston singing "I Will Always Love You" began to play. Though Houston was never perfect, she will always be loved—loved by her family, her friends, and her legions of fans.

———•◆•———

Bobbi Kristina

Houston left her entire estate to Bobbi Kristina, who was 18 at the time of her mother's death. The money will be placed in a trust until Bobbi Kristina turns 21. At that point, Bobbi Kristina will receive a portion of the money, with more to follow when she turns 25 and 30. In a televised interview with Oprah Winfrey that aired one month after Houston's death, Bobbi Kristina said she was doing as well as she could under the circumstances. She plans to carry on her mother's legacy by pursuing a singing and acting career.

TIMELINE

1963

Whitney Elizabeth Houston is born on August 9 in Newark, New Jersey.

1981

As a model, Houston appears on the cover of the November issue of *Seventeen* magazine.

1983

Houston signs a recording contract with Arista.

1988

Houston performs at London's Wembley Stadium to celebrate antiapartheid leader Nelson Mandela on June 11.

1989

Houston launches the Whitney Houston Foundation for Children.

1990

I'm Your Baby Tonight, Houston's third studio album, is released in November.

1985

Whitney Houston, Houston's debut album, is released in February.

1986

Houston wins her first Grammy Award for Best Pop Vocal Performance, Female for "Saving All My Love for You."

1987

Whitney, Houston's second album, is released in June and debuts at Number 1 on the *Billboard 200* album chart.

1991

Houston performs the "Star-Spangled Banner" at Super Bowl XXV in Tampa, Florida, on January 27.

1992

Houston marries Bobby Brown on July 18.

1992

Houston plays pop star Rachel Marron in *The Bodyguard*, her first feature film role.

IMELINE

1993

Houston and Brown's daughter, Bobbi Kristina Houston-Brown, is born on March 4.

1994

Houston wins three Grammy Awards for *The Bodyguard* soundtrack, including Album of the Year.

1998

My Love Is Your Love, Houston's fourth studio album, is released.

2002

Houston sits down for an interview with ABC newswoman Diane Sawyer.

2002

Houston's fifth studio album, *Just Whitney*, is released.

2007

Houston and Brown's divorce is finalized.

2000

Security personnel
at a Hawaii airport
discover marijuana
in Houston's
carry-on luggage
on January 11.

2000

*Whitney: The
Greatest Hits* is
released in May.

2001

Houston signs
a $100 million
contract with
Arista in August.

2009

I Look to You
is released.

2011

Houston produces
and costars in a
remake of the 1976
movie *Sparkle*. She
plays the mother of
an aspiring singer.

2012

Houston is found
dead in the bathtub
of her hotel room in
the Beverly Hilton
on February 11.

DATE OF BIRTH
August 9, 1963

PLACE OF BIRTH
Newark, New Jersey

DATE OF DEATH
February 11, 2012

PLACE OF DEATH
Los Angeles, California

PARENTS
John and Emily "Cissy" Houston

MARRIAGE
Bobby Brown (1992–2007)

CHILDREN
Bobbi Kristina Houston-Brown

CAREER HIGHLIGHTS

Selected Albums

Whitney Houston (1985)
Whitney (1987)
I'm Your Baby Tonight (1990)
The Bodyguard (soundtrack) (1992)
My Love Is Your Love (1998)
Whitney: The Greatest Hits (2000)
Just Whitney (2002)
One Wish: The Holiday Album (2003)
I Look to You (2009)

Films

The Bodyguard (1992)
Waiting to Exhale (1995)
The Preacher's Wife (1996)
Rogers & Hammerstein's Cinderella (television) (1997)
Sparkle (posthumous release) (2012)

QUOTE

"I don't sing music thinking this is black or this is white. . . . I sing songs that everybody's going to like."—*Whitney Houston, 1990*

 GLOSSARY

backup singer
> A singer who provides vocal accompaniment for the lead vocalist on recordings and in live performances.

chart
> A weekly listing of the current best-selling records.

crossover artist
> A singer or musician whose work appears simultaneously on multiple music charts, such as R&B and pop, and appeals to listeners with a variety of musical tastes.

debut
> A performer's first formal concert or recording.

gospel
> Spiritual music that originated in African-American churches in the South.

mezzo-soprano
> A woman's singing voice that is lower and darker than a soprano.

New Jack Swing
> A type of music popular in the mid-1980s to the mid-1990s that blended elements of R&B, hip-hop, and dance club pop.

producer
> Someone who oversees or provides money for a play, television show, movie, or album.

R&B

A type of popular music with roots in jazz, blues, and other urban musical genres.

record label

A company that manages a band's music, particularly in regards to producing, manufacturing, distributing, and marketing albums.

single

An individual song released by a band for play on the radio.

 ADDITIONAL RESOURCES

SELECTED BIBLIOGRAPHY

Houston, Cissy, with Jonathan Singer. *How Sweet the Sound: My Life with God and Gospel.* New York: Doubleday, 1998. Print.

Parish, James Robert. *Whitney Houston: The Unauthorized Biography.* London: Aurum, 2003. Print.

"Whitney Houston Tells All: Transcript of Interview with Oprah Winfrey, 14 Sept. 2009." *Oprah.* Harpo Productions, n.d. Web. 7 May 2012.

FURTHER READINGS

Durkee, Cutler. *People: Remembering Whitney Houston: A Tribute.* New York: Time Home Entertainment, 2012. Print.

Sullivan, Robert, ed. *LIFE: Whitney 1963–2012; A Tribute.* New York: Time Home Entertainment, 2012. Print.

WEB LINKS

To learn more about Whitney Houston, visit ABDO Publishing Company online at **www.abdopublishing.com**. Web sites about Whitney Houston are featured on our Book Links page. These links are routinely monitored and updated to provide the most current information available.

FOR MORE INFORMATION

For more information on this subject, contact or visit the following organizations.

The Grammy Awards

www.grammy.com
Houston was awarded many Grammys throughout her career. Visit the Grammy Awards Web site for information about her and other musicians.

Whitney Houston Official Web Site

www.whitneyhouston.com
Visit Houston's official Web site for news, images, and other information about the singer.

SOURCE NOTES

Chapter 1. America's Sweetheart
1. "Whitney Houston Sings The National Anthem—The Star Spangled Banner." *YouTube*. YouTube, 25 Apr. 2007. Web. 25 Apr. 2012.
2. J. A. Adande. "Getting Vocal about Anthems." *Los Angeles Times*. Los Angeles Times, 3 Oct. 2001. Web. 25 Apr. 2012.
3. Gil Kaufman. "Christina Aguilera Apologizes for Super Bowl National Anthem Flub." *MTV News*. Viacom, 7 Feb. 2011. Web. 25 Apr. 2012.
4. "Whitney Houston: The Super Bowl May Have Been a Doozy, but the Best Moment of All Came Right before Kickoff." *People*. Time Inc., 30 May 1991. Web. 25 Apr. 2012.

Chapter 2. Nippy
1. Cissy Houston with Jonathan Singer. *How Sweet the Sound*. New York: Doubleday, 1998. Print. 162.
2. Ibid. 170.
3. Mary Shaughnessy. "Whitney Houston's a Chip Off the Old Pop Diva." *People Weekly* 9 Dec. 1985. *Classic Whitney*. Web. 25 Apr. 2012.
4. Cissy Houston with Jonathan Singer. *How Sweet the Sound*. New York: Doubleday, 1998. Print. xiii.
5. Ibid. xiv.
6. Ibid. xv.
7. Bud Scoppa. "The Long Road to Overnight Success." *Billboard Magazine* Dec. 1986. *Classic Whitney*. Web. 25 Apr. 2012.
8. Ibid.
9. Cissy Houston with Jonathan Singer. *How Sweet the Sound*. New York: Doubleday, 1998. Print. 229.

Chapter 3. A Superstar Debuts
1. "Whitney Houston—Live on Merv Griffin Show." *You Tube*. YouTube, 3 Mar. 2011. Web. 25 Apr. 2012.
2. Ibid.
3. Richard Corliss. "The Prom Queen of Soul." *Time* 13 July 1987. *Classic Whitney*. Web. 25 Apr. 2012.
4. Don Shewy. "*Whitney Houston*." *Rolling Stone*. Rolling Stone, 6 June 1985. Web. 25 Apr. 2012.
5. Ibid.
6. Cissy Houston with Jonathan Singer. *How Sweet the Sound*. New York: Doubleday, 1998. Print. 231.
7. Dennis Hunt. "Baker and the Rise of Black Women in Pop." *Los Angeles Times*. Los Angeles Times, 18 Jan. 1987. Web. 25 Apr. 2012.

8. Tom Green. "Whitney Houston, Ready to Return to the Groove; Whitney's New Ways." *USA Today* 30 Oct. 1990. *Classic Whitney*. Web. 25 Apr. 2012.

9. Cissy Houston with Jonathan Singer. *How Sweet the Sound*. New York: Doubleday, 1998. Print. 229.

10. Ibid. 231.

Chapter 4. She Does It Again

1. Vince Aletti. "*Whitney*." *Rolling Stone*. Rolling Stone, 13 Aug. 1987. Web. 25 Apr. 2012.

2. Richard Corliss. "The Prom Queen of Soul." *Time* 13 July 1987. *Classic Whitney*. Web. 25 Apr. 2012.

3. Dolores Barclay. "In the Groove: Record Reviews *Whitney*." *Associated Press* 8 July 1987. *Whitney-Fan.com*. Whitney Fan, n.d. Web. 25 Apr. 2012.

4. Tom Green. "Whitney Houston, Ready to Return to the Groove; Whitney's New Ways." *USA Today* 30 Oct. 1990. *Classic Whitney*. Web. 25 Apr. 2012.

5. Joy Duckett Cain. "The Soul of Whitney." *Essence* Dec. 1990. *Classic Whitney*. Web. 25 Apr. 2012.

6. "Whitney Houston Uses Fame to Help Good Causes." *Jet Magazine* 20 June 1988. *Google Book Search*. Web. 25 Apr. 2012.

7. Ibid.

8. David Van Biema. "Whitney Houston." *Life* Oct. 1990. *Classic Whitney*. Web. 25 Apr. 2012.

9. Ibid.

10. Anthony DeCurtis. "Whitney Houston: Down and Dirty." *Rolling Stone* 10 June 1993. *Classic Whitney*. Web. 25 Apr. 2012.

11. Ibid.

Chapter 5. Something in Common

1. Anthony DeCurtis. "Whitney Houston: Down and Dirty." *Rolling Stone* 10 June 1993. *Classic Whitney*. Web. 25 Apr. 2012.

2. Ibid.

3. Robert Hilburn. "How Cruel Can Fame Be, Bobby Brown?" *Los Angeles Times*. Los Angeles Times, 27 Sept. 1992. Web. 25 Apr. 2012.

4. Anthony DeCurtis. "Whitney Houston: Down and Dirty." *Rolling Stone* 10 June 1993. *Classic Whitney*. Web. 25 Apr. 2012.

5. Ibid.

6. Tom Green. "Whitney Houston, Ready to Return to the Groove; Whitney's New Ways." *USA Today* 30 Oct. 1990. *Classic Whitney*. Web. 25 Apr. 2012.

Source Notes

CONTINUED

7. James Hunter. "*I'm Your Baby Tonight*." *Rolling Stone*. Rolling Stone, 10 Jan. 1991. Web. 25 Apr. 2012.

8. David Browne. "Music Review: *I'm Your Baby Tonight*, Whitney Houston." *Entertainment Weekly*. Entertainment Weekly, 23 Nov. 1990. Web. 25 Apr. 2012.

9. Robert Hilburn. "How Cruel Can Fame Be, Bobby Brown?" *Los Angeles Times*. Los Angeles Times, 27 Sept. 1992. Web. 25 Apr. 2012.

Chapter 6. A Big Role, A Big Song, A Big Day

1. Lynn Norment. "Whitney Houston: Model, Singer, Actor, Wife, and Mother to Be." *Ebony* Jan. 1993. *Classic Whitney*. Web. 25 Apr. 2012.

2. Anthony DeCurtis. "Whitney Houston: Down and Dirty." *Rolling Stone* 10 June 1993. *Classic Whitney*. Web. 25 Apr. 2012.

3. Ibid.

4. Lynn Norment. "Whitney Houston: Model, Singer, Actor, Wife, and Mother to Be." *Ebony* Jan. 1993. *Classic Whitney*. Web. 25 Apr. 2012.

5. Cissy Houston with Jonathan Singer. *How Sweet the Sound*. New York: Doubleday, 1998. Print. 232.

6. Anne Trebbe. "Feeling Like a Princess: Whitney Houston's New Life." *USA Today* 5 May 1992. *Classic Whitney*. Web. 25 Apr. 2012.

Chapter 7. Behind the Mask

1. Owen Gleiberman. "Movie Review: The Bodyguard." *Entertainment Weekly*. Entertainment Weekly, 4 Dec. 1992. Web. 25 Apr. 2012.

2. Janet Maslin. "The Bodyguard: Tragic Flaw Meets Pampered Pop Star Over Multiple Risks." *New York Times*. New York Times, 25 Nov. 1992. Web. 25 Apr. 2012.

3. Roger Ebert. "The Bodyguard." *Chicago Sun-Times* 25 Nov. 1992. *RogerEbert.com*. Web. 25 Apr. 2012.

4. "Interview with Dolly Parton." *Larry King Live*. CNN, 3 July 2003. Web. 25 Apr. 2012.

5. Meredith Berkman. "Pregnant Pause." *Entertainment Weekly*. Entertainment Weekly, 5 Feb. 1993. Web. 25 Apr. 2012.

6. Lynn Norment. "Whitney Houston: Model, Singer, Actor, Wife, and Mother to Be." *Ebony* Jan. 1993. *Classic Whitney*. Web. 25 Apr. 2012.

7. Ibid.

8. Vince Aletti. "Look Who's Ticking." *Village Voice*. Village Voice, 8 Dec. 1998. Web. 25 Apr. 2012.

9. Ibid.

10. Lynn Norment. "Whitney Houston: Model, Singer, Actor, Wife, and Mother to Be." *Ebony* Jan. 1993. *Classic Whitney*. Web. 25 Apr. 2012.

Chapter 8. Falling Star

1. Larry Katz. "Getting Intimate with Whitney." *Boston Herald* June 1999. *Classic Whitney.* Web. 25 Apr. 2012.

2. "Mariah Talks About Whitney Duet, Takes Stage With Jermaine Dupri And Da Brat." *MTV News.* Viacom, 31 Aug. 1998. Web. 25 Apr. 2012.

3. Lynn Norment. "Whitney Houston: Model, Singer, Actor, Wife, and Mother to Be." *Ebony* Jan. 1993. *Classic Whitney.* Web. 25 Apr. 2012.

4. Ibid.

5. Isabel Wilkerson. "God Is Still Working on Me." *Essence* July 2003. *Classic Whitney.* Web. 25 Apr. 2012.

6. "Whitney Houston Tells All." *Oprah.* Harpo Productions, 14 Sept. 2009. Web. 25 Apr. 2012.

7. "Transcript: Whitney Houston: I'm a Person Who Has a Life." *ABC News.* ABC News, 4 Dec. 2002. Web. 25 Apr. 2012.

8. Ibid.

9. Ibid.

10. Ibid.

11. Ibid.

Chapter 9. One Day at a Time

1. "Whitney Houston Booed as US Tour Opens to Mixed Reviews." *Popcrunch.* Popcrunch, 14 Apr. 2010. Web. 25 Apr. 2012.

2. "Whitney Houston Owes Comeback to Daughter." *Sky News.* BskyB, 24 July 2009. Web. 25 Apr. 2012.

3. "Whitney Houston Tells All." *Oprah.* Harpo Productions, 14 Sept. 2009. Web. 25 Apr. 2012.

4. Ibid.

5. Phil Gast. "Jakes: 'Sparkle' Remake Would Have Relaunched Houston's Career." *CNN.* Cable News Network, 17 Feb. 2012. Web. 25 Apr. 2012.

6. Amy Kuperinsky. "Whitney Houston Funeral: A Galaxy of Stars Honor One of the Brightest." *NJ Star-Ledger.* New Jersey On-Line, 19 Feb. 2012. Web. 25 Apr. 2012.

7. Shirley Halperin. "Whitney Houston Funeral: Read Clive Davis' Eulogy in its Entirety." *Hollywood Reporter.* Hollywood Reporter, 18 Feb. 2012. Web. 25 Apr. 2012.

8. "Whitney Houston's Funeral: Love and Humor Dominate Remembrances of Pop Star." *NJ Star-Ledger.* New Jersey On-Line, 18 Feb. 2012. Web. 25 Apr. 2012.

9. "From Beyonce to Gaga: 8 Singers Influenced by Whitney Houston." *ABC News.* ABC News, 16 Feb. 2002. Web. 25 Apr. 2012.

NDEX

ABOUT THE AUTHOR

Christine Heppermann is a columnist and reviewer for *The Horn Book Magazine.* Her nonfiction picture book *City Chickens* will be published by Houghton Mifflin in 2012. She has also published poetry in literary journals for adults. She has a master of arts degree in Children's Literature from Simmons College and a master of fine arts degree in Writing for Children and Young Adults from Hamline University.

PHOTO CREDITS